KU-167-263

St Vincent
and the
Grenadines

St Vincent and the Grenadines

Photography by Mike Toy
Text by Kathy Martin

MACMILLAN
CARIBBEAN

Macmillan Education
Between Towns Road, Oxford OX4 3PP
A division of Macmillan Publishers Limited
Companies and representatives throughout the world

www.macmillan-caribbean.com

ISBN 0 333 93415 6

Text © Kathy Martin 2003
Photographs © Mike Toy 2003
Maps © Macmillan Publishers Limited 2003

First published 2003

All rights reserved; no part of this publication may be
reproduced, stored in a retrieval system, transmitted in any
form or by any means, electronic, mechanical, photocopying,
recording, or otherwise, without the prior written permission
of the publishers.

Designed by Gary Fielder at AC Design

Printed and bound in Malaysia

2007 2006 2005 2004 2003
10 9 8 7 6 5 4 3 2 1

Contents

Acknowledgements and Technical notes

The images in this book are a product of many trips to the islands over a period of several years. It would simply be impossible to mention everyone who has helped along the way. But helped they have and without them this book would not have been possible. There are those individuals who have graciously allowed me to photograph them; those who have allowed me access to their factories and workplaces; hotels and resorts that have fed and watered me and countless people who have provided directions, insights, explanations and suggestions. My sincere thanks go to you all. And special/particular thanks to Kelly Glass for providing air transport and Lavinia Gunn for her endearing, and enduring, hospitality.

All the images in this book were shot on Fujichrome slide films, namely Velvia and Provia F. The vast majority were shot with Nikon cameras and lenses, the exception being some of the architectural and interior photographs that were shot with Hasselblads.

Acknowledgements from Kathy Martin

In writing the text for this book I have drawn on the accumulated wisdom of so many former pupils, colleagues and friends as well as the work of other researchers and recorders, often from centuries ago. To single out one or two would be to do a disservice to many but I do thank them. Much information was made available through the helpful services of Ms Youlou Griffith at the National Archives. Mr Jeremy Gunn and Ms Mary Barnard provided photographs from our past. I would also like to thank the Vincentian poets or their heirs for allowing me to weave some of their words into the picture book. For checking the final manuscript I am indebted to Dr Earle Kirby and my ever-supportive husband, Cims.

Preface

I have tried to touch a little on all aspects of the huge variety of life and land that make up St Vincent and the Grenadines (SVG). I shall admit to being lucky that I live a short plane ride away and have visited the country many times, both for work and for pleasure. Many of the images in this book come from other assignments – the villas of Mustique for example – and have allowed me to show things that might otherwise not be seen. Not everyone is going to go to Mustique; not everyone is going to be in Bequia for the Easter Regatta or Kingstown for Carnival.

But they are all an integral part of life in SVG. Each of the islands is different and has its own special character and feeling. Some I know well; others I have spent only a few brief hours on. No doubt if you look around you will see things I have not, but in the meantime I hope this book will afford a good look at what is certainly one of the most beautiful of the Caribbean nations.

A quiet spot near Chateaubelair.

1

Introduction to ...

St Vincent and the Grenadines

If one day you sail to the end of the world, following your dreams, seeking a place where it is always warm, and the skies are blue, yet there is clean, fresh water to drink; a place with coral sands and silvered, azure seas, brimming with fish, where dolphins play, yet there are verdant valleys yielding fruit; where there is a fiery volcano with gritty grey flanks and lush tropical gardens with humming birds sipping nectar from the flowers; a place which invites you to rest amidst the palms or hang out on a toe-strap as your boat catches the breeze; a place where people smile and say 'hello'. You could say 'You can't have it all' or you could say 'You are in St Vincent and the Grenadines'.

Sunrise

Tear me a piece of morning
pristine
crisp
unwrapped from a silver sunrise.
Mix me a few pastel notes of
Birdsong.
Toss me a fine brush of
ocean spray
and I'll paint you a wet poem
and lean it against
a new Caribbean sky
to dry.

From *Note to the Unseen* by Peggy Carr.

St Vincent and the Grenadines

Straddled across the 13th parallel near the intersection of the 61st western meridian, St Vincent and the Grenadines form part of the Windwards in the Lesser Antillean chain of islands. The Grenadines consist of some 40 islands and cays which represent the emerged peaks of the Grenadine Bank. For the most part this bank runs northwards from Grenada at about 20 to 30 fathoms depth (37m to 55m) and stops abruptly at Bequia. It was formed in the Eocene period 60 million years ago, of pillow lavas pushed out of the molten interior of the earth where the Caribbean crust meets the Atlantic. Since then it has undergone several alternating cycles of coral limestone formation and volcanicity. St Vincent, 18km further north across the 600-fathom deep Bequia Channel, was much more recently formed of volcanic rocks from the late Pliocene onwards, over the last 3 million years.

The first people known to have lived in St Vincent and the Grenadines were the Siboney, a pre-ceramic, Stone Age culture. They were followed by waves of other Amerindian peoples migrating up through the islands towards what today is Puerto Rico. Scientists note these migrations occurred roughly every four hundred years and seem to coincide with Mega-Niño events. The enhanced El Niño is thought to disrupt weather patterns round the world and in northern South America it may have caused severe droughts and fires which triggered migrations. Pottery shards, petroglyphs, stones ground into mortars and sharpening tools give tantalising clues to how these ancient ancestors of ours lived. The earliest carbon date we have obtained so far is 160 AD ±100 years. This was from a pink conch shell *(Strombus gigas)* dug out of an old kitchen midden where the Kingstown Post Office now stands. The pottery pieces found with it are from the Pearls series of the Insular Saladoid cultural period. They are remarkable for their high quality clay mix, good firing and fine-grained temper. Red, white and black patterns were often added together with perhaps crosshatching or delicate flanging. Animal adornos denoting the spirit of the pot were frequently fashioned as lug handles on bowls and vessels. These lugs would cool rapidly

The marks of passing people have been left as petroglyphs throughout the land. This 6m tall 'sacrificial stone' near Layou is thought to bear the triangular imprint of Yocahu, the God who brought cassava to the people.

so that the pot could be handled as the fire burnt down. Griddles for making cassava bread are plentiful and ceremonial ware is represented, of which the most striking example is the two-foot high bat stand fished out of the Greathead river in Arnos Vale by Janet Wall and reassembled for the National Museum collection by our father of archaeology, Dr Earle Kirby.

By the year 1000 AD the Caliviny culture of the Arawak Indians had largely replaced the Saladoid and this in turn gave way to the Suazey from 1200 AD. This was the time the Calinagos arrived from Galibi on the Maroni River in the Guianas. The Arawak blood and customs were preserved through the women who consorted with these fit, adventurous newcomers. There is strong evidence to suggest that the Calinagos found St Vincent and the Grenadines the most attractive and fruitful of the Antillean islands and made it their headquarters. Certainly they were there when Columbus voyaged through the region. Incidentally the name St Vincent dates from that time. During the European battles for colonies in the West Indies that followed, the Calinagos held their own in St Vincent for several centuries. Britain and France were forced to agree by treaty in 1660 and again in the Treaty of Aix-la-Chapelle in 1747, that St Vincent belonged to the Caribs. However, time was running out for the Calinagos. Many had intermingled with Blacks to produce the Black Calinagos. The origin of these black people is controversial. Some believe they arrived in the fourteenth century when King Abubakari's expedition came across from Mali aided by the Canaries Current. Some say they escaped from a shipwrecked slaver off Bequia in 1675. Whoever is right it was the Black Calinagos who, aided by the French, mounted a fierce resistance to the British when they took away their ancestral lands after the

And here at Indian Bay Point, chiselled in the massive rock, a similar figure with arms akimbo.

Treaty of Paris in 1763. This culminated in the Calinagos driving out the enemy and reclaiming their estates on both sides of the island. Eventually the British were marooned in Kingstown and Fort Charlotte. It was only then that, by virtue of more advanced technology arriving by sea, coupled no doubt with the ravages of European and African diseases, the Black Calinagos were routed. Their leader, the Paramount Chief and probably Joseph Chatoyer, St Vincent and the Grenadines' first national hero, fell in battle arguably to the sword

The patterns of the petroglyphs, particularly the ones at Yambou and Barrouallie have inspired the shape of the marker signs at the entrance to the villages.

of a British major in a duel at Dorsetshire Hill on 14 March 1795. His people, the Black Calinagos, were deported to Roatan island on the Honduran Coast. Happily their descendants, the Garifuna people, now have rediscovered their roots and return from time to time. The 'Yellow' Calinagos who did not fight the British remained on lands beyond the Dry River and groups of Black Calinagos who evaded deportation made their home in Greiggs.

The yellow Calinagos or Galibi were settled North of the Rabacca Dry river.

These children live in the village of Greiggs where Galibi blood still runs through many a vein.

The next generation lines up for school.

The new Greiggs Primary School was opened in April 2000 as a model school for the twenty-first century.

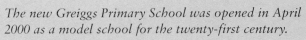

Classrooms are light and
airy and look out onto
green fields and gardens.

The children look to the
future with confidence.

St Vincent and the Grenadines

The plantation economy prospered and at its zenith produced more sugar than any other island in the British Antilles except Jamaica. The cost of this was 24 out of 25 people living in slavery. Today you can see vestiges of Ashanti, Yoruba, Ibo as you walk the streets. Meetings are still held under the almond tree in African tradition on Bequia. In the culinary field, cod, imported by the ton as cheap food for the workforce, from Boston, New England, has been transformed into a much loved delicacy, Buljol, and which Vincentian does not like to come home to a good pigtail soup? Tall casuarinas mark the entrance to once great houses and fig trees thrive in the lime used to cement old boiling house walls near the ruins of sugar mills which mark the skyline.

Slavery was abolished in 1838 and immediately the country was plunged into a labour crisis as former slaves withdrew their services from the plantations. East Indians, fleeing poverty in Madras and Calcutta, were indentured to fill the shortfall. They stayed on the island and the beautiful banana fields of Richland Park are a tribute to their subsequent endeavours. Our curried goat and delicious split pea roti are resonant of India. Meanwhile on the island of Madeira another human tragedy was unfolding. Famine followed the drought which caused the vine and potato crops to fail and starving Portuguese people opted to migrate. They were so glad of the opportunity to work that they often pushed themselves too hard. Occasionally some would die

Peter's Hope has been earmarked for possible hotel development. In 1828 some 101 Black slaves produced 195,000 lbs of sugar and 7200 gallons of rum on this 400-acre estate.

Renewable energy. This water wheel once used to power a sugar factory.

in the cane fields so the planters tended to employ them in the workshops and running the estate store. Ever thrifty, many ran small businesses, particularly in the food and drinks area and in housing development.

The fear of insurrection always worried the planters. The imperialist maxim of 'Divide and rule' seemed to be working. It was for this reason that another group was welcomed to St Vincent and the Grenadines. These were Scottish captives from the Duke of Monmouth's rebellion in 1685. They settled

So did this old windmill at Harmony Hall.

'When I grow up I want to grow bananas. Now I help carry the boxes to pack them in'.

in Bequia, Gordon Yard and Dorsetshire Hill. Some of these people, gravitating to the cooler slopes, were able to benefit from small mixed farms. Nowhere in the whole of the country are fields so neatly terraced to conserve the soil. The land is contoured with hand hoes to create a patchwork of crops: sweet potatoes, carrots, cabbage. If you go up Dorsetshire Hill on a Sunday, look out for the playing field and, as elsewhere in the country, you are quite likely to see a game of cricket in progress. It was a point of burgeoning national pride when the first English team touring the West Indies was soundly beaten by a wicket and 76 runs at Victoria Park in 1895.

Commodity prices are notoriously volatile. St Vincent and the Grenadines has coped in a variety of ways. The Grenadines turned to the sea. The men often sailed on the bulk carriers and brought money home to invest in houses and businesses. The fish of course was needed to feed the family but its profusion and quality, free of the heavy metals of more polluted waters, meant that it found its way to the dinner tables and restaurants of Martinique. Offshore banking and information technology are making a growing contribution to the economy.

A welcome extends to you from the kitchen door.

Tall tall Moko Jumbie bois bois will be on the road soon.

That great explosion of Carnival Bacchanal occurs here every July. It has its origins in the pre-Lenten masked balls of the French planters but it was the ordinary people who took it as their own. The revellers would assemble in central Kingstown and each group, accompanied by string band, bamboo flute, 'goat skin' bom drums and their own kaiso singer, would parade to Government House to perform for the Administrator and his friends at the Botanic Gardens. A wooden pole (sceptre) and crown were awarded to the winners who became king or queen for the day. Calypso tents of bamboo and coconut leaves were set up for the bands to hold 'dress rehearsals' prior to their Shrove Tuesday presentations. The town buzzed with anticipation as character acts mixed with onlookers awaiting the bands. There were dragons and donkey bands, bois bois and boosey back, stick fights and maypole dancers and the stately quadrille. And look out! Monkeyman would strain at his chains and black up your clothes if you did not give him 5 cents.

The Harmonites String Band keeps the crowd in the street bar entertained.

A steelband, one of the
quintessential elements of the
Caribbean carnival.

'He sketched then painted me
Me pouring on the keyboard of my pan,
My drumsticks poised to loosen melodies
My arched wrists near the circle of steel'

From *Portrait of a Panman* by Owen Campbell.

The streets turn into pure 'ol' mas' on J'ouvert morning.

Character portrayals are part of the fun at J'ouvert.

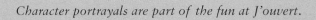

Revellers take to the streets smeared in green mud. If you get in close you might get muddy too.

It is Carnival Tuesday and Dinks Johnson's band, Wizards, has already left the tent.

Since 1946 a carnival committee has organised this event. Today, events are staged across the country culminating in a 10-day festival in Kingstown. The excitement first begins to build up as band leaders announce their themes and display drawings of the costumes each section will wear. You might have chosen to join 'the Dynasties of ancient Egypt' with Roy Austin's Bridgeboys or 'Seasons' with Avis Yorke. Nelson Bloc are ready or maybe 'Nonsense story – mouth open 'tory jump out' as Roy Ralph's Dragons draw you in. So off you go to sew your costume. Meanwhile, back at the tents (large buildings have now displaced the bamboo and coconut) wirebenders are busy into the early hours each night, crafting the headdresses and the king and queen costumes take shape. Further down the block a would-be socca monarch would be working out his lyrics and the calypsonian would be weaving local events into the rubric of this year's calypso – the best often a little bit naughty and full of innuendo. The Halls of Fame include Lord Lorenzo, Mighty Sheller, Professor MBE, Caribbean Hawke and many many more. Steelband music drifts across from the panyard where Vinlec Potential or Starlift are practising. Beauty queens arrive from the other islands to compete for the Miss Carnival crown. The action comes thick and fast. Junior carnival, pan competition, calypso finals, king and queen of the bands, carnival queen show and then it is J'ouvert morning. This is 'ole mas' of class, when word play and impersonation hold sway. The joke can be on anyone amidst a swirling mass of t-shirt bands and mud dancers jumping up in the street to the heady beat of the latest socca tunes. Carnival Tuesday, the old Mardi Gras, sees the bands parading, section by section, across the stage in Victoria Park and on to the streets to jump up. Who will get band of the year? Who will get road march? Lord Hawke got it with 'Sweeter than this', Becket with 'Wine down Kingstown', 'Touch with Jam them', and what about 'Somebody's woman'?

Magnificently costumed individuals converge on Victoria Park.

Interestingly, a cultural tradition developed at the Christmas season, which is unique to St Vincent and the Grenadines. This is the Nine Mornings Festival. Beginning on 16 December and continuing until Christmas Eve, the young and young at heart get up out of their nice warm beds in the early hours, or indeed do not go to bed at all. They find their way onto the streets of town to jump and dance, such is the magnetic draw of drum beat and pulsating 'blocko' music. No one is quite sure how the custom began but it is thought that slaves, waiting to take their masters home from church at the Yuletide season, may have been the first Nine Mornings revellers.

Masqueraders wait to go on stage to be judged, section by section, band after band. Here is a children's section.

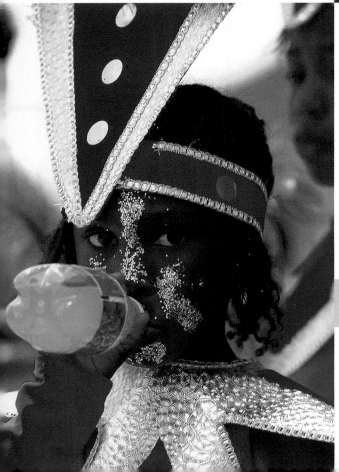

Just time for a shot.

Fantastic!

Competition is hot for Queen of the Bands.
*Jacintha manoeuvres this shimmering costume
to the delight of the crowds.*

*On stage the masqueraders
burst into life, dancing,
jumping and 'win'ing'.*

A piece of the action from the band 'Shake dat Cocktail', a Mirage production.

'Music in me blood and
rhythm in me bones'

The rather grand Georgetown Methodist Church. It was rebuilt in 1903 after a hurricane destroyed the 1870 structure.

Christmas is a magical time with homes aglow with fairy lights. Vincentians coming home from New York each year bring this Latin American tradition with them. The Roman Catholic Church facade in Kingstown is particularly beautifully lit at this time. Church bells ring in celebration and carol singers spread festive cheer raising money for the needy. Kitchens are redolent with baking hams and blackcake, ginger beer and sorrel. Little fingers are stained green as the children help to shell pigeon peas to go with rice and hope that this has not escaped Santa's attention.

Yes, the churches play their part well now, and Sunday morning sees people dressed in their finest to attend services in the traditional Roman Catholic, Anglican and Methodist churches or in the more recently arrived Pentecostal ones. This however was

not always so. The first Methodists arrived in 1787 and in 1793 Mr Lamb, a Wesleyan preacher, overstepped official practice by preaching to Blacks. He was imprisoned for his crime. Despite efforts of the planter class to deculturalise the slaves, fragments of African religions and beliefs survived into the twentieth century. Before electrification it was difficult to believe a jumbie spirit would not get you if you passed near the cemetery at night and who was sure a soucouyan would not escape from his skin and come to drink blood before the cock crew? This was an event dreaded by small boys who had to collect water at the village standpipe and carry it home on their heads for early morning tea. Each village had its healer in those days and many people still drank concoctions like shine bush tea for their high blood pressure. Nowadays we see pharmaceutical products such as aloe shampoo and

In a place where everybody knows everybody else, processions are very much a part of community life.

And a procession usually means a wayside preacher.

noni juice using some of the same herbs. Death rituals also have vestiges of earlier beliefs. The mourner's 'belly' may be banded and hanging pictures and mirrors turned to the wall so as not to hinder the spirit of the departed as it is sung joyfully on its way.

Food is brought to the house for nine nights of 'set up' and at the 40- and 100-day wakes which marked the dead person entering the spirit world of the ancestors and tribal deities. Much of African religious practice was expressed in the Shaker religion and so afraid of this was the establishment that it was only in the 1940s that the Spiritual Baptist Church was given the right of freedom of religion. Rastafarianism similarly promotes the African heritage.

We have an anchor that keeps the soul

Steadfast and sure while the billows roll;

Fastened to the rock which cannot move.

Grounded firm and deep in the Saviour's love!

From *Will Your Anchor Hold?* by Priscilla Jane Owens.

Lower Bay is the venue for a good part of the spectacular Easter Regatta.

The Grenadines have so far featured as the spearhead of tourist development in SVG. There is an airport on Canouan and airstrips on Bequia, Mustique and Union Island. The islands are provisioned by sea and there are scheduled passenger services by motor vessels to Kingstown. Holiday accommodation is largely in upmarket hotels and resorts. The product is the exquisite white coral beaches that you have to share with the passing sandpipers, the clearest crystal waters through which to view the reef and stupendous turquoise bays to drop anchor in after a day of running before the trade winds. The most perfect peace and serenity is broken only by the cacophony of crickets as they conduct their nightly chorus signalled by the burnished rays of the setting sun.

Culturally then, St Vincent and the Grenadines is a glorious melange of Africa, Asia and Europe in America. The various elements have blended into an attractive easygoing people who are, nevertheless, able to hold their own on

Maybe when the sun rose
for the first time
he was just too timid to shine
lest he couldn't do it.

From *Challenge* by St Clair Jimmy Prince

the world stage out of all proportion to their numbers. You will scarcely go to any country where a Vincentian does not pop up. They helped to dig the Panama Canal, cut cane in Cuba and the Dominican Republic, pumped oil in Aruba and Curaçao, staffed the transport services and hospitals of postwar Britain, provided professional services for Canada and plugged the labour shortages in New York City, filled professorships in the USA and trained artisans for the rest of the Caribbean. They fought in two world wars. Vincentians strengthen the football and athletics teams of many countries not to mention our own Pamenos Ballantyne, the top ranking Caribbean long distance runner and Olympic hopeful. Together with our sister islands, our music is now worldwide and we have carnivals in several North American and British cities, the pre-eminent being Labor Day in Brooklyn, USA, and Notting Hill carnival in London, UK.

The government of the island has also changed much over the years, from chiefdom to colony to independent state. Universal adult suffrage was achieved in 1952, largely through the efforts of George McIntosh and his working men's association. In the elections which followed, for the first time a democratically elected party, led by Comrade Charles, represented the majority of the people in the House of Assembly. He was followed by Chief Ministers Ebenezer Joshua, after whom the main airport is named, and Milton Cato to whom the hospital is commemorated. Milton Cato became the first Prime Minister when he led the country to independence from Great Britain in 1979 with a parliamentary system modelled on Westminster. Sir James Mitchell, Mr Arnhim Eustace and the present incumbent, Dr Ralph Gonsalves, followed him. The country is a member of the British Commonwealth and the head of state is Queen Elizabeth II. Her representative is the Governor General.

2

*Indian Bay, its golden sands and azure
sea make it a favourite swimming spot.*

St Vincent

*St Vincent has always been a special place ever since the grumbling earth first spat her
forth into the glistening blue sea through myriad volcanic vents. It is the last island in
the Caribbean to be born, the youngest, the most desirable, the most beautiful.*

Let us journey through St Vincent. We will start way up in the North Leeward so we'll need a boat. This is the Falls of Baleine, 20m of cascading water just a 10-minute scramble over the rocks from the sea. The plunge pool is big enough to have a party in or you can sit on the ledge behind the waterfall and muse.

St Vincent

I ndeed, the oldest rocks to be dated so far are those outcropping in Villa. Here basaltic dykes and lava flows extruded in the late Pliocene era some 3.5 million years ago, at about the same time that humankind is thought to have evolved in Africa. Mesopotamia was formed 3.4 million years ago. The island gets progressively younger northwards, Mesopotamia 3.4Ma, Grand Bonhomme 3.0–2.0Ma, the Richmond Peak Mt Brisbane complex 1.9–1.2Ma and of course La Soufrière which is still active today. This volcano began as a stratified cone of alternating lava flow and pyroclastic deposits. It then went through a series of Plinian explosions, which destroyed the summit and enlarged the crater. The next phase was a quiet one with more lava flows and pyroclastic material. Increased explosivity from the magma chamber, estimated to be 15 to 20km below the crater floor, has been noted in recorded history. The first documented eruption was in 1718. In 1812 a new crater was formed to the northeast of the old one. The eruption of May 1902 sent steam clouds 10,000m high into the atmosphere and killed 1600 people. 1971 brought further activity when an island appeared in the crater lake. The most recent eruption, on 17 April 1979, blew that island to smithereens.

The heritage of this formative activity is a breathtaking scenery of rounded volcanic peaks and sharp spined ridges dropping dramatically to the flat valley floors. At the coast these valleys are encroached on by the sea creating bays lined with glowing black sand. This landscape is further enhanced by a mantle of lush green vegetation. Rainfall varies between 2,050mm and 3,800mm yearly according to location. The wetter parts of the island, particularly the Windward side, have an optimum natural vegetation of tropical rainforest with dominant 30-metre tall Gommier (Dacryodes

excelsa) and buttressed Santinay (Sloanea caribea) trees. This still exists in the Vermont valley where a nature trail has been laid out and in Colonarie Basin. Elsewhere hurricane, volcanic eruption and land clearance for agriculture have impacted and much of the woodland which does remain is secondary. You can often be walking through what you might think is primeval forest when you come across a breadfruit tree left back from somebody's yam patch. Above 500m the forest shrinks to elfin woodland with epiphyte and moss laden trees to 4m or, in exposed spots, palms. Over on the Leeward side of the island the slopes gradually turn golden as the dry season progresses and the forest prepares to shed leaves. It is at times like this that the cactus scrub on the coastal rocks survives best.

Where the Wallibon waters meet the sea,
Soufrière sits sulking, solitary, swathed in mists.

I shall go down to the sea
whence cometh my love.
In her crystal, clear waters
I see myself reflected
and I smile
for
the gently lapping waves
caressing the black sand.
They remind me of my loved one.

From *The Seas* by Al T. Daisy.

Refreshment is on hand at Richmond Beach. The Nice Time Inn has been recently enlarged to help you with your picnic needs.

Fishing boats at Petit Bordel.

Seine nets hanging out to dry in Barrouallie. The town is also well known for the blackfish or pilot whale, which are harpooned there.

The traditional pretty little board house is increasingly rare these days. Originally the design had been used in the American colonies and came to St Vincent after Barbados adopted it. Each house was constructed from prefabricated sections and raised off the damp ground on pillars. The 'chattel' house could be taken apart and reassembled elsewhere when the occupier's workplace changed. Typically these 3m by 6m houses had a door in the long side and sash windows or shutters with hoods and jalousies to keep them cool. The roof was steeply pitched and often decorated with 'gingerbread' under the eaves. The one in the picture has been extended by adding a lean to roof over the porch.

Table Rock is a great picnic spot.

Because the vulcanicity is so recent and ongoing, weathering has produced very fertile yellow and brown earth soils. The very best soils formed on newly breaking rock are to be found on the steepest slopes which may be difficult to cultivate. This is a fact known only too well to village farmers lucky enough to have inherited some 'mountain lands' to grow their provisions: tannia, yams, eddoes, sweet potatoes and more recently cabbage and other green crops.

The flatter lands were generally reserved for cash crops and therein lies a tale. These lands were cleared as a condition of sale to British planters in the eighteenth century. King sugar prospered with many people migrating from the other islands to work the remarkably productive lands of St Vincent. When sugar prices fell, other crops were introduced. Arrowroot, originally brought by the Caribs and grown in the gardens of freed slaves, was cultivated extensively and the sugar factories were converted to arrowroot processing units. Many of us remember, as children, eating madungo bakes, madungo being the starch skimmed from the top of the arrowroot settling tanks during crop processing. The sea island cotton, introduced in 1903 was world renowned for quality. By 1944 arrowroot made up 50 per cent of total exports, sea island cotton 23 per cent and cacao, syrup and sugar 18 per cent and falling. Today, bananas are the most important crop, many of them propagated by tissue culture. They are shipped to England green and ripened on arrival. Ground provisions and vegetables are traded to other Caribbean territories and a veritable profusion of fresh local food is available on the market stalls.

The Vermont valley is a good place to stop off for a river dip. Is Table Rock nearby? The gardened settlements in this luxuriant valley have won the 'Best Village' competition on several occasions.

Ah here's Table Rock. Just time for a quick wash. What a boon the river was in the drought of 2001!

This rainforest trail takes you through a section of the parrot reserve where you can actually view these rare and beautiful birds in their natural habitat. Recent estimates of population size suggest there are only about 600 Vincentian parrots left in the wild. They are now conserved under The Wildlife Protection Act of 1987.

Vincie is the national bird of St Vincent and the Grenadines. Its primary feathers sport the colours of the nation's flag, blue for the sea and sky, gold for the warmth of the people, the sun and the sands of the Grenadines and green for the lush vegetation.

The flora and fauna we have is very much a matter of chance. After the eruptions seeds were carried to colonise the new lands, by wind, sea or animals. Half came from Central America down the island chain and half from South America dispersing northwards. Alfred Wallace, nineteenth-century traveller, collector and evolutionary biologist records seeing a large boa constrictor snake arriving on St Vincent's shore 'twisted round the trunk of a cedar tree, and was so little injured by the voyage that it captured some sheep before it was killed'. On that occasion the snake successfully dispersed but failed to establish itself. Fortunately other boas (the Congo snake, *Corallus hortulanus*) were not so ill fated and together with the white snake *(Mastigodryas bruesi)* and the endemic black snake *(Chironius vincenti),* have established breeding colonies. They are all harmless to people and help

The Forestry Department runs a breeding project in the Botanic Gardens where rescued birds are given shelter. So far some 24 chicks have been hatched at the aviary. The adults were DNA tested recently to work out which birds could contribute best to the gene pool.

The Botanical Gardens, founded in 1765, are the oldest in the western hemisphere. They were established to introduce, test, propagate and distribute tropical crops and ornamental plants to the Americas and as such they are one of the most important gardens of all times.

Captain Bligh was reputed to have been a cruel captain. His first efforts to bring breadfruit from Tahiti, in 1789, resulted in himself and some 1,000 young breadfruit trees being cast adrift in the Pacific during the mutiny on the Bounty. Breadfruit were successfully given into the care of the St Vincent Botanic Gardens at his second attempt.

keep down the numbers of less desirable migrants, such as mice and rats. Several single island endemic species exist today. Exclusive to this island and nowhere else are a whistling frog species *(Eleutherodactylus shrevei)*, the tree lizards *(Anolis trinitatis* and *Anolis griseus)*. *Anolis trinitatis* is the blue/green/yellow fellow you will probably see running over your terrace. Of the avifauna, the whistling warbler (*Catharopeza bishopi*) and our national bird the St Vincent parrot (*Amazona guildingii*) are indigenous. The native population of mammals consists of nine species of bat and of course humankind. The bats play a major role in pollination and seed dispersal as well as insect control. There are four other mammals: the mongoose *(Herpestes auropunctatis)*, the nine-banded armadillo *(Dasypus novemcintus)*, the agouti *(Dasyprocta antillensis)* and the manicou or opossum *(Didelphis marsupialis)* which is the only marsupial outside Australasia. The mongoose was introduced to control rats in the cane fields. The rat, however, soon learnt to climb trees and would look back at the mongoose applauding its vain attempts to follow. The hungry mongoose turned its attention to depleting the dove population and then it discovered chickens.

Torch lily (Phaeomeria magnifica). *This magnificent 1 to 1.5m tall flower is dwarfed by its 3m leaves.*

Breadfruit trees (Artocarpus incisa) *were planted throughout the land to provide food.*

Shrimp (Pachystachys lutea) *a genus native to the American tropics.*

This ixora is a hybrid of Ixora coccinea, *native to tropical Africa and India. The name 'ixora' comes from a Malabar deity.*

Probably the most showy of the hundred or so native orchids belonging to the genus epidendrum. This is the fragrant Epidendrum ciliare *which is much sought after by collectors.*

*I have forgotten much
but still remember
the poinsettia's red,
blood-red, in warm
December.*

From *Flame-heart* written with
nostalgia for his Caribbean home
by Claude McKay.

The century palm in bloom.

The oldest botanical garden in the new world flourishes in Kingstown. It was established in 1765 to receive and propagate economic and horticultural plants brought from the East Indies. St Vincent was selected for this garden because it had the best soils and most agreeable climate in the region with temperatures averaging between 24°C and 30°C. The exotic plants multiplied and it was from here that they were distributed to the American tropics. Gold medals were awarded by the Royal Society in England to encourage this transfer. Dr Young, the garden's first superintendent, was awarded a gold medal in 1773 for having 140 healthy cinnamon, mango and nutmeg trees amongst other things. Today, cut flowers, particularly hybrid anthurium lilies, are exported to flower shops in the metropolitan countries and experimentation continues with orchid cultivation. The garden itself is a magical microcosm of all the tropical gardens in the world.

Young Island, named after Sir William Young who headed a commission to St Vincent after it was ceded to Britain in 1763. He certainly had an eye for a bit of good real estate.

As night draws on you can dine at one of the small hotels along the romantic Villa beach. The view across the water casts a spell, so beware! If it is Friday night it is 'culture pot' in the fishing village of Calliaqua just round the corner. Once you hear the music you are bound to want to stop in and party.

Dining al fresco at this 5-star luxury hotel, Young Island was developed as St Vincent's first tourist resort hotel by John Hauser in the 1960s. Prior to this, John had been responsible for developing Hilton hotels throughout the region. Two Vincentians, Dr Freddie Ballantyne and Mr Vidal Browne are now the owners.

Above the tennis court at dusk you can often spot agouti and iguana taking their evening feed. These animals are protected on Young Island.

The bar lies stretched out along the sands, between the natural rock face and the gently lapping seawater. Well known personalities like the Beatles and Bill Gates have enjoyed a famous Young Island Special cocktail here.

The idyllic pool is set in lush tropical gardens. One or two of the cabanas are hidden away nearby.

Syl De Freitas is buried inside that white cross. It is as though he is sitting there surveying the beautiful Villa area beyond which he developed.

The Point, Young Island and Rock Fort circa 1901. On the Point was a cotton drying house, built on the site of Wilkies Battery. This later became the Grand View Hotel.

The Point, Young Island and Rock Fort in 2001. Sandwiched between the blue Caribbean Sea and green hills, the Arnos Vale sports stadium is reported as being the most attractive location in the Caribbean for a game of cricket.

Across the runway, at Arnos Vale 2, a cricket match is in progress.

Georgetown was once a thriving sugar town. The shipping wharf is no more, but these galleried houses, built out over the pavement at the end of the nineteenth century, remain.

Holy Trinity Church, Georgetown dates back to 1823.

Tri-tri are caught in sheet traps set in river mouths round the island. These tiny fish are West Indian white bait suckstone. The eggs hatch as they wash out to sea and the hatchlings migrate back up the river three nights before the new moon. Fried Tri-tri cakes make an excellent lunch.

Park at Argyle and listen to the rocks being ground
ever rounder by the might of the wild Atlantic rollers.

Like a natural jacuzzi the bubbling surf conditions the magical black sand beaches of the Windward coast.

A bamboo grove marks the end of the road. From here an exhilarating two-hour climb through liana clad forests and out onto the cinder cone will take you to the top of the volcano.

The Rabacca river washed so much ash and scoria down from the denuded Soufrière peak after the eruptions that its lower reaches became clogged up and dry. The Rabacca sands from the Dry river are used as a building aggregate.

Graceful tree ferns mark the transition between forest and the flowers and moss of the mountain top.

The 1812 eruption of La Soufrière, from a painting by J. M. W. Turner, based on a sketch by Hugh Keane.

The thing split Good Friday in two
and that good new morning groaned
and snapped
like breaking an old habit.

From *La Soufrière* by E. McG. 'Shake' Keane.

The crater lake from a drawing by the
Revd W. Bouchier in the Illustrated
London News *of 17 May 1902.*

In 1976 an island could be seen
emerging from the lake. The
island and lake were blown sky
high on Good Friday 1979.

This is what was left of La Soufrière after the eruption on 17 April 1979.

La Soufrière, looking down into the sulphurous crater in 2001. The cone in the centre is slowly growing day by day.

A brooding landscape waiting …

The pulp is strained and the starchy liquid left on the sedimentation table to settle. The starch is then dug out and loaded onto trays like the one being carried here.

But life goes on ... Domino!

And some people have to work:
Arrowroot rhizomes arrive at the factory in Owia where they are washed and pulped.

Arrowroot flour makes delicious cakes. Its use in biscuits and as a thickening agent for sauces is well known. It has been used to provide a fine finish on computer paper.

A farmer in Mesopotamia goes to feed his cows.

Bananas growing on Collins Estate in the fertile Marriaqua Valley. These are the Robusta variety, which have good preservation properties, enabling them to withstand the long passage to England. Bananas provide a weekly income to small farmers throughout St Vincent.

Perfect hands of bananas are put in boxes in the field and sent to the Kingstown wharf.

Blue plastic bags protect the developing bunches against damage from biting insects like thrips.

Planting bananas. When a new sucker is planted it will take nine months to bear fruit.

Up, up and away onto the Geest banana boat bound for Southampton, UK. Look for the WIBDECO label when you buy your bananas.

NOTICE
TO ALL
PERSONNEL
SAFETY GLASSES
MUST BE WORN
AT ALL TIMES
WHEN BREAKING
BOTTLES.

cn TAKTINA

Hairoun

And to quench that after-work thirst, what better than a locally brewed Hairoun beer, fresh from the bottling line?

Staff receive training. Key personnel study right up to Master Brewer level in Germany.

These local chives are going to be made into hot and spicy seasoning using Ms Erica McIntosh's secret recipe. She received the 'Caribbean Entrepreneur of the Year 1999' award from the Organisation of Eastern Caribbean States (OECS).

Cigarettes on the transfer drum ready for packaging in the factory at Casson Hill.

The new filter tips are aimed for the export market.

Maritime traditions have resulted in a pool of ship servicing skills in the country. Here a boat is being cleaned up ready for repainting at the Ottley Hall dry dock.

Layou is another of the fishing settlements on the Leeward coast.

St Vincent has six small towns. Georgetown in the North Windward was the hub of the last thriving sugar industry. It is a nice place for a meal after you have climbed the volcano. On the Leeward coast lie Chateaubelair and Barouallie which, as their names suggest, were prominent in the French era. Further south is Layou. Like all the Leeward settlements Layou depends on fishing. The waters are calm and particularly clear because the black sand contains magnetite which sinks readily. Swimming from these beaches of magnetic sand has the benefits of a health spa treatment. The southernmost towns are Kingstown and Calliaqua.

Kingstown, situated on a bay which provides an excellent sheltered anchorage, is the capital. The encircling hills lent themselves to the defence of Kingstown. Batteries were set up at Sion Hill and Dorsetshire Hill in addition to the Fort, named after Queen Charlotte, the wife of George III. Fort Charlotte once had some 34 cannons, mostly

pointing inland. A path linked it with Government House should the ruling elite have needed refuge. The battlements provide a splendid 360° lookout point.

79

Kingstown in 1902.

The House of Assembly passed a resolution to erect this Georgian Courthouse in 1798. It is an imposing building with its triple arched entrance to the loggia. White painted plaster quoins pick out the corners, arched lower windows and the upper windows with their Demerara shutters. The ground floor houses the Court of Law whilst the Legislature occupies the upper level. In times past it was also used for grand balls and concerts.

The bustling town today.

Always impeccably dressed, the police constable
carries his uniform with distinction. His cap badge
bears the St Vincent and the Grenadines coat of arms
with the inscription 'Pax et Justitia'.

The Illustrated London News of
24 September 1898 showed the Police
Barracks and Courthouse. The
Barringtonia asiatica tree next to the
river flowing through the market square
was one of several which lined the
Bayfront and are believed to have come
from Madagascar.

The Police Barracks in Kingstown is an imposing stone
building completed in 1875 to replace an earlier one
destroyed in the great fire of 26 October 1866. Built in
a style modelled on the courthouse, it features elegant,
jalousied windows. Red and yellow clay bricks are
used to highlight windows and to form a decorative
course through the middle and top of the facade. The
arched entrance to the central parade ground is topped
by a flagpole and, on the roof, a decorative
octagonal tower.

81

And of course Middle Street has its rum shops.

The cool interior of St George's Cathedral. The church was consecrated in 1820 after the previous one was destroyed by a hurricane in 1780. It stands in spacious grounds in a prime location on Back Street in keeping with its status at that time as the established church of the land. No permanent buildings were put up on St George's Place then, so that guards at the courthouse gate could see when processions moved from the church gate heading for the courthouse for the civil part of the proceedings.

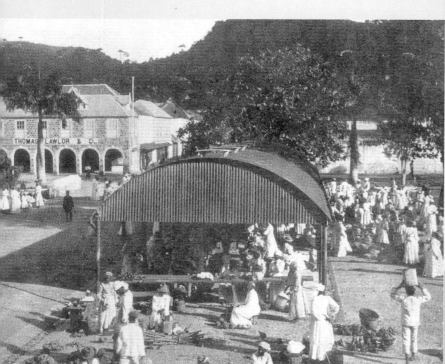

The French, with their unfailing sense of the aesthetics laid out the original square. Almond, silkcotton and tamarind trees provided shade and greenery at that time.

82

Middle Street, between Back and Bay Streets, retains the quaint dimensions laid out by the French in the eighteenth century. A rummage through the shops lining it today can yield practically anything: a cutlass, New York fashion, bolts of cloth, a kerosene oil lamp, even an 'olde tyme' flat iron.

Protective shingle covers many traditional style houses which have boarded walls or roofs. They were cut from timber like the bitter red cedar which could resist the weather and termite attack.

Kingstown itself is perhaps most characterised by its attractive arched colonnades which shade the cobbled pavements below. This is a rare feature outside the Spanish islands of the Caribbean. The Bay Street, which was originally laid out along the shoreline, is edged with historic old merchants' warehouses dating from 1765. They were built from local volcanic stone and red and yellow clay bricks brought as ballast in the holds of sailing ships. There are several fine Georgian buildings in the town. The old library, the courthouse and St George's Anglican Cathedral are worth a special look. Many of the older dwelling houses are typical of French Creole architecture to be found across the region right up to New Orleans. They have thick stone ground floor walls and wooden walls above. Jalousies direct the breeze into the rooms exactly where you want it. The lacy 'gingerbread' roof edging, once typical of these houses, is to be seen decorating many of the attractive new Vincentian homes today. Business has expanded in the town over the years and in the service sector particularly. There are some excellent little cafés and restaurants tucked in amongst the courtyards and back streets just waiting to serve up a cool drink, local mauby or a callaloo soup. A stop at one of these is a must if you are in town.

Red clay bricks were commonly used for decoration in Kingstown. They came from Europe as ballast on the old sailing ships.

The new Kingstown Market opened in 2000. A bountiful supply of fresh fruit and vegetables overflow into the central rotunda.

Here, squeezed onto the bank of the North River, and at least once washed away by it, stands the Roman Catholic Cathedral of the Assumption. Together with the adjoining St Mary's Primary School, charming courtyards, fountains and presbytery, it was fashioned over two centuries in an amazing blend of Flemish, Moorish, Venetian, Byzantine, and even Romanesque architectural styles.

The Caribs would not recognise
Ooashegunny Bay today. The
Kingstown waterfront has moved
some several metres out to sea as
a result of a land reclamation
scheme in the 1970s and deep
water wharves have been
constructed for trade and
cruise ships.

*A cruise ship awaits the return of its passengers who
are being taken on scenic day tours from the dock.*

And now it is time for us to go on
board too. The mail boat will
take us down the Grenadines.

'*Goodbye St Vincent, Goodbye Mount St Andrews, we are off to Bequia*'.

MV Admiral I *alongside. Passengers and supplies arrive in Port Elizabeth from St Vincent.*

Bequia

A place where time stands still.

On Sunday morning there is barely a seat to spare.

Bequia

A short journey across the water from St Vincent lands you in another world, which is why SVG is such a superb tourist destination. It has so many different things to offer known only to the local people and a few very select visitors. As you set foot in Bequia you relax into its gentle, friendly pace. You learn to walk again and saunter slowly to the bakery for fresh 'homemade' bread. You collect some vegetables from the market stall and call a greeting to people you meet. Maybe you stop by a bayside bar for an iced passion fruit juice and perhaps have a swim before you walk back to your home. Slipping under the trees, as you go up the hill, you check to see if the little teacup and saucer mangoes or the sapodilla are ripe. Some cashew and Bequia plum stew would be nice if plums are in season. Later on you might go to meet the fishing boat when it comes in and buy some red snapper for dinner.

Like the rest of the Grenadines, Bequia is much lower and less forested than mainland St Vincent so rainfall is light. It averages 1000mm a year. Each house has a large tank into which water, collected from the rooftop, is stored ready for the dry season, normally from January to May. In really dry years a sea bath is exactly that and water is kept for drinking only. The forest too learns to adapt and, depending on the thickness of the soil, may be a xeric woodland dotted with the waxy white flowers of wild frangipani *(Plumeria alba)* and the pendulous lilac bells of cedar *(Tabebuia heterophylla).* These trees offer perches to a big, noisy, chicken-like bird whose onomatopoeic name is the cocrico *(Ortalis ruficauda).* They are thought to have been introduced here and in Union Island from Tobago in

the late seventeenth century. Another interesting introduction was the tortoise *(Geochelone carbonaria)* which can be spotted wandering ponderously through the undergrowth, perfectly at home with the pace of life. Lizards are plentiful, including the island endemic dwarf gecko *(Sphaerodactylus kirbyi).* Differences between ground lizards *(Ameira ameira)* from one island to another are reminiscent of variation in the Galapagos finches. Now if only Darwin had stopped here!

Someone who did make Bequia his destination was a Mr Warner, and he came, in 1762, to grow sugar. His lands passed by marriage to Sir William Wallace who retired from the British navy in 1830 to manage the Friendship Estate. The Hazell family, by dint of hard labour, worked their way up to acquire Cinnamon Gardens, Park, Spring and Industry.

The main town of Bequia is Port Elizabeth on Admiralty Bay, seen here from Old Fort.

It is the ideal place for children.

Turn left from the jetty and you will come to Seargent Brothers' model boat shop.

The gifted craftsmen turn these gum trees into …

… these wooden hulls which, once painted and fully rigged, are ready for racing. Many visitors buy them as souvenirs of the friendly, seafaring people of Bequia they have met.

St Mary's Anglican church, built of Bequia limestone in 1829, offers a place for cool contemplation right on the waterfront.

After emancipation, labour was in short supply and owners, as elsewhere in the colony, often returned to England leaving managers to run the estates. There was a shift from sugar to cotton in Bequia and, as the population declined, subsistence cultivation of pigeon peas and corn, together with stock rearing, increased. By the late nineteenth century, Joseph Ollivierre, of French descent, still had 789 acres at Paget Farm including Isle Quatre, Savan and Petit Nevis. Various people of Scottish, Irish and Portuguese descent had been able to buy land. The McIntoshes, originally estate managers, had the old Hazell lands, the Simmonses, Happy Valley and Lower Bay; the Peters had Diamond. William Scott was in control in Hope, Camel, Union, and Paradise, John Mascoll at Mt Pleasant and Miss Syllena at Hamilton.

It was Moshe and Bill, two sons of William Wallace, who started Whaling in Bequia. The tradition was handed on to Athneal Ollivierre, who used his Petit Nevis lands as a whaling station. In a tussle of man against nature the little wooden boats would venture out to intercept the humpback whales *(Megaptera novaeangliae)* in their spring migration. If luck was with the whaler the hand held harpoon would hit its target and hold. Then the battle began as the little rowing boat, perhaps rigged with a sail, was dragged after the whale. As it became tired the whale could be landed and conch blowing would summon Bequians to help haul it ashore and take a welcome share of the meat. Today the International Whaling Commission allows SVG to kill four whales per year under the aboriginal hunting clause.

A stroll along the Belmont walkway will take you past several delightful family run hotels like the Gingerbread.

Some have pools like Plantation House.

And if you continue, you can climb over the point to enjoy a secluded swim from the sparkling white sands of Princess Margaret Beach.

These cool open air taxis, available on VHF68, are usually waiting on the waterfront.

It is a brilliant ride over to Park Bay at the end of the road.

At Park Beach you can visit the Old Hegg Turtle Sanctuary. Brother King has rescued hundreds of these increasingly scarce little hawksbills. When they are six years old he releases them back into the wild.

Heading in the opposite direction you come to Paget Farm and the Whaling Museum. 125 years of humankind, whales and the elements are chronicled within these walls.

Further along the road at the First and Last Bar, it is time for a drink.

Conservation is also the name of the game over on Park Beach. As the Wider Caribbean Sea Turtle Conservation Network (WIDECAST) publicises the plight of sea turtles, Orton King has established his Oldhegg Sanctuary. It is here that you can view hundreds of hawksbill turtle hatchlings being fattened up for release back into the wild.

Boat building had its heyday in the late nineteenth and twentieth centuries. More Vincentian boats were built in Bequia than anywhere else using the plentiful and durable timber from the cedar trees.

Building on this seafaring tradition, and with tourism in mind, the Bequia Sailing Club organises an Easter Regatta. This four-day event has drawn the international yachting crowd in to race ever since its inception in 1967 and the atmosphere of the clubhouse spills all over the island. Each day brings a different event, be it the fishing boat race, round the island race or, what boys of all ages enjoy, the model coconut and gumboat races. Shoreside activities are a real barrel of fun with competitions in sandcastle building, limbo dancing, tug-o-war, backgammon and not forgetting the crazy craft.

An alternative holiday can be had at Moonhole if you rent one of these houses carved into the cliff. Moonhole is named for the view of the moon through this natural rock arch from Paget Farm.

The Regatta is an annual extravaganza organised for the past 35 years by the Bequia Sailing Club. It attracts competitors from the Caribbean area and beyond.

GOOD NEWS

The Lower Bay beach is awash with
colour as fishing boats await their races.

Into the twenty-first century.

Bequia fishing boats are characteristically double ended.

Preparing to launch a fishing boat for the Easter Sunday race.

And they are off racing past Moonhole!

The junior league await their turn.

Yacht under sail in the Bequia Channel. It could be the Round the Island Race.

The yachting crowd is ashore in Port Elizabeth now, their bum boats left at the jetty.

Here is the Commodore checking out the waters.

After the fun of the regatta, Bequia sinks back into sleepy serenity again.

Steel band music entertains the crowds at Lower Bay on Easter Sunday.

But for us the Friendship Rose *is waiting. Calvin Lewis and the Adams brothers built this wonderful old wooden schooner in Bequia in 1966. She did the mail run between Union Island and St Vincent for many years and is an absolute dream to sail with. Let us go!*

Elegant boutiques on the shores of Britannia Bay embrace elements of creative creole style both in the fashions within and the decorative 'gingerbread' architecture outside.

4

Mustique

Playground of the rich and famous, there are no paparazzi in Mustique. Whew!

Flamboyant, and we do not mean a house. The magnificent
Delonix regia, *makes a big splash in June and July.*

Mustique

So just what is it that attracts the super rich to holiday here? Well, it all started when the island was bought by the flamboyant Lord Glenconner, then the Hon. Colin Tennant. Hailing from a wealthy industrial background his family had been involved in chemicals, engineering and beer. He was checking on family assets in Trinidad, where the Tennants had been absentee sugar planters since the nineteenth century, when he heard that the Hazells were selling an island. In 1958 he sold the family's remaining estate in Trinidad and purchased Mustique. The island's residents were offered a lump sum if they wished to leave or they could opt to stay and work with the new owner.

After an initial flight of fancy with cotton, Colin turned to tourism. He presented his friend Princess Margaret with a 10-acre plot as a wedding present and this gift was to give the island a certain cachet. Sketches for Princess Margaret's house were drawn up by stage set designer Oliver Messel, her then husband's uncle. Oliver teamed up with Hugo Money-Coutts who had been at Eton with Colin Tennant and was to manage affairs. In the cavalier manner typical of his class, Hugo learnt to fly in just two weeks and brought a light aircraft down on the cricket pitch in Mustique, thereby solving the immediate access problems. He next flew off to Petit St Vincent. Mustique needed a builder and he knew where to find one. He returned with Arne Hasselqvist who started converting Oliver's imaginative designs into structurally sound and very attractive homes. This triumvirate was to get Mustique off the drawing board.

The Mustique Company, set up in 1968, had planning permission to build up to 140 houses on the 1400-acre island in addition to the village which was already there. An airstrip was opened the following year and the cotton warehouse on the old Endeavour Plantation site was converted into a top class hotel. Colin Tennant ran Mustique in his own idiosyncratic way, more like a private estate than a company. Snippets of news were slipped to the press notwithstanding the general policy to protect the privacy of the high profile guests. Soon Nigel Dempster's 'Mustique Diary' in the gossip column of the 1970s *Daily Mail* was to regale Britain with the naughty shenanigans of the celebs on holiday. This was no mean draw! With money no problem, a stream of well-travelled people indulged their dreams

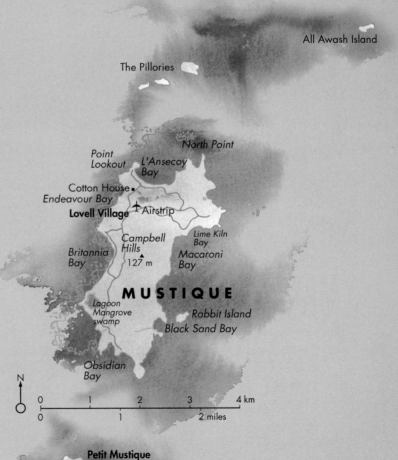

'Mustique, exclusive but not excluded' to borrow a phrase coined by Colin Tennant. And what better place to begin than the village school at Lovell. It was designed, built and donated by Arne Hasselqvist in 1984. Some 24 children are on the register. The Mustique Education Trust holds a very popular annual barbecue at Macaroni Beach to help in fundraising for the school. They also assist students who go on to Bequia or St Vincent for secondary education as well as supporting adult education classes and a fine library open to all.

on the island. There were international pop stars like Mick Jagger and David Bowie, aristocrats and industrialists like the Guinnesses. Patrick Lichfield was there and the more recent arrival of international bankers and entrepreneurs included fashion designer Tommy Hilfiger. Villas appeared in fantasy styles culled from countries round the world: Balinese, Provençal, Japanese, British colonial, Moroccan, classical Italian and, not forgetting with naturally, Caribbean.

A consortium of home owners now controls the company and is following a policy of limited development and environmental protection. Some 90 spacious luxury houses have been built so far and only 30 more are envisioned so that the seclusion and tranquillity of each is preserved. Golf courses are definitely taboo as is further hotel development. Brian Alexander, manager for more than 20 years, claims there is over a billion EC dollars invested in Mustique and from this EC$55 million goes into the Vincentian economy yearly, mainly in wages for the 1,150 Vincentian employees. The Mustique Company in turns gets generous tax concessions. Brian feels upmarket tourism is the way to go for our little islands. It brings a small number of visitors to impact on the environment but each one makes a substantial financial contribution once a quality product is available.

The eighteenth-century Cotton House interior after Oliver Messel's sensitive conversion to a hotel. He retained the coral stone walls and enhanced the traditional tray ceiling with a dusting of lime.

Jacaranda is one of an identical pair of British colonial type houses on L'Ansecoy Beach. Its builder, Arne Hasselqvist, using ideas he had absorbed from Oliver Messel, designed it. In true Messel style an invitation to the beach extends right through the house.

And from the beach, a quick dip in the pool will freshen you up on your way back to the house.

She who touched the tide and flow of our lives with the quiet force of her steadying hand

From *My Mother's Faith* by Travers Phillips.

Chalice vine or cup of gold (Solandra nitida) native to Central and South America.

117

Now let us see if anyone is home here.
This is the door to Frangipani.

No, nobody about,
but what an eyeful
from Frangipani's
terrace! Just the
place to relax.
I wonder if this is
one of the 50 or so
homes up for rent
when the owner is
not around. If you
do not use it you
lose it or so they say.

Away from the manicured lawns and swimming pools there is still much to cherish. The fifteenth-century Spanish sailors used to call the island Los Pajaros, meaning 'the birds'. One of the best sites to spot them is the swamp and mudflats bordering L'Ansecoy Bay. It is a treasure trove of herons, seven or eight species, coots, plovers and sandpipers. Many migrants call in to refuel on their journey to northern nesting grounds and can be seen in March and April. Northwards from the beach you can see Baliceaux, the name, a corruption of 'Petit Isle des Oiseaux', little island of birds. The magnificent frigate bird *(Fregata magnificens)* is recorded as having breeding colonies there. Wild cows lived in the dry forest on Mustique but have not been seen for a few years now. There is, however, an interesting cave where bats hang in the day and on Black Sand Bay, in September, nurse shark *(Ginglymostoma cirratum)* have been seen giving birth. Of course, the marine life is superb as the Bequia fishermen know only too well. They come to camp on Britannia Bay and set their purse-seines when schools of fish swim up to the beach as the moon rises.

The calm waters of Britannia Bay have always provided the anchorage of choice. It is for this reason that the bayfront remains the focus of activity on Mustique to this day. Let's move in closer.

Colourful double ended Bequia fishing boats are pulled up on the northern end of the shore. If you go down to the beach on a moonlit night as the moon rises you might see the men hauling in the seine. The fish market just nearby gives island residents the chance to sample the catch. Lobsters, in season from 1 September to 31 March, are a real delicacy.

Basil's Bar is the place to eat out informally. Its charismatic owner, Basil Charles, is a Biabou man made in Mustique where his charm and wit have earned him a place in the lives of the homeowners.

A range of activities for the young and young at heart are available on Mustique as on all the 'tourist' islands: windsurfing, snorkelling, tennis, horse riding and not forgetting scuba diving through spots like the Pillories. And everybody ends up, sooner or later, for a sundowner and a glimpse of the green flash at Basil's Bar.

Over on the breezy Atlantic coast, hanging above Lime Kiln Bay, like an osprey's eyrie, is the house Discovery.

About turn and
we have views
southwards as far as
Macaroni sands.
Natural boulders
are an integral
feature of this house
and water-worn
pebbles tile the
pool, embracing the
warmth of the
afternoon sun into
the evening.

Are you ready to dine?

How is this for a central place? The elegant drawing room is a focal point in Zinnia. Separated from the dining area by grand Doric columns yet unified with the simplicity of Messel inspired white on white, it is the perfect place to pass the port after dinner.

Or perhaps you prefer to catch the slanting rays of the tropical evening sun on the terrace. Zinnia is located in the centre of the island, with sweeping views across country.

Then it is upstairs to dreamland, or am I there already?

Here we are at one of the jetties. Canouan has some brilliant beaches!

5

Canouan

'Cannoun', is the island of turtles which came to breed in the soft sands, in harmony
with our Amerindian forebears for centuries.

This is one of the signature colours of the Carenage Bay Resort. Would you like to go in?

Canouan

Folklore gives this small island a colourful history of piracy and lawlessness. It is thought that the Amerindian tribes may have made fairly temporary encampments here on their way north. If this is so, the buccaneers of the eighteenth century could well have found the island uninhabited and a suitable refuge to return to with plunder reaped in 'deeds of daring do' on the high seas. Could Bachelors' Hall have been the pirates' lair?

William Snagg was one of the first English planters to buy land in Canouan. Initially he grew sugar at Carenage. Sugar prices however, collapsed and this affected him in two ways. Firstly, he was able to buy out lands further south and hence came to own virtually the whole island. Secondly, he switched from sugar to the production of Marie Galante cotton. His son James, in an effort at diversification, reverted to the crops the Caribs had once cultivated: cassava, peas, sweet potatoes and corn. James set up house with a remarkable woman, a slave called Pink. They lived at the Great House which formed part of a complex consisting of a church, a village, storehouses and water cisterns at Carenage. In 1838 Benjamin Compton, a shipwright from Hampshire, UK came to build boats for James Snagg and in so doing started an industry which thrived for years in the Grenadines. Boat building and whaling were inextricably linked. It was Henry Snagg, the eldest of the seven children Pink bore James, who began whaling from Rameau Bay. Jonathan Lewis did the same for a number of years from Rumereng Bay. Meanwhile Benjamin Compton's two children spawned the Mitchell and Compton family lines which were to produce two Prime Ministers. Sir James Mitchell served in SVG and Sir John

Compton in St Lucia during the closing decades of the twentieth century.

Gradually the Canouan estate became unprofitable and it was sold to the government in 1946. The village, destroyed by a hurricane in 1921, was relocated on Grand Bay to suit the new fishing and sailing orientation of the people. This meant that much of the island reverted to nature. The acacia thorn scrub, the vegetation to emerge, was disturbed only by cattle and goats.

Soon the natural beauty of this idyllic place was spotted and delightful small hotels like the Canouan Beach Hotel and Crystal Apartments opened their doors. CBH offers catamaran day charters in with the price. The airstrip facilitated easy access.

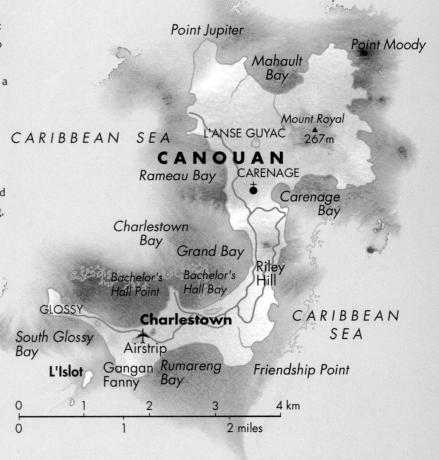

A yacht at anchor at Manhault Bay.

The Tamarind Beach Hotel recently opened on Charles Bay.

In the 1990s something happened that was to change the face of Canouan forever. The northern half of the island was leased to the Canouan Resort Development Company. Today the land is sculptured into an 18-hole golf course, three tennis courts, a swimming pool and a network of access roads for the use of hotel staff and patrons. A series of gold and blue painted accommodation units provide 240 suites and a further 48 rooms are available in the beach hotel. These together with the Beach Club buildings were designed by the famous Italian architect Luigi Vietti. Then of course, for that extra little bit of excitement, there is the exclusive Big Point Casino. The old Anglican Church survived the 1921 hurricane and the developer's bulldozers to remind us of yesterday.

The 18-hole (par 72) Frangipani golf course named after the indigenous tree which still finds a toehold hanging onto the steep sea cliffs.

Carenage Bay Resort.

The view across Grand Bay from Batchelor's Hall Point is stunning. Most of the Canouan people have this view for breakfast at their homes in Charlestown.

The South Glossy Bay beach spreads out before you like a crystal carpet as you step from your room at the Canouan Beach Hotel. This view is towards Taffia Hill, Gangan Fanny and L'Islot.

They are traditionally fisher folk.

MV Barracuda, *the mail boat, comes in to dock. Let us go aboard. Roll-on, roll-off ferry boats made a huge difference to the Grenadines when they were introduced in the 1970s.*

Walk up through the village and you will find this pretty little Roman Catholic church on top of the hill.

6

Mayreau

Mayreau – pure, unspoilt gem.

At Mayreau Garden hard corals abound. In this picture you can see yellow pencil coral, finger coral and sheet coral.

Mayreau

Mayreau remains awe-inspiringly beautiful with its horseshoe bays and picture book shores. Its rich marine life has earned the tranquil northeast corner a place in the National Marine Park.

It is thanks to the conservative approach of its present owners, the Eustace family, that it remains largely untouched by the modern materialist world. The Eustaces are descended from the St Hilaire family which was closely associated with the Empress Josephine. They had to flee France at the time of the Revolution. The village still remains from the old cotton growing days but each villager now owns the title deed for his or her own house plot. This was an important development for two reasons. Firstly, no would-be developer can ever remove them from their ancestral land as has happened in some islands and secondly, the deed can be used to raise investment capital for home improvements, business or education. You can now get a delicious meal of fresh seafood at one of the restaurants along the village street and even arrange to stay overnight.

Reverence for the ancestral spirits is one of the African traditions, which has been kept alive in Mayreau through the Feast of the Parent Plate. A concrete tombstone is made to mark the passage of a year since a loved one departed. On the day before, rice, peas, flour and livestock are solicited from the villagers. The Minister blesses the food and formerly, when the goats were killed, blood would be sprinkled to all four corners of the deceased's home to deter evil spirits coming back with the loved one. In recent times it has been discovered that rum also works quite well. Women then cook the food. In the old days the pot, often a tin oil can, would have been rested on three stones which made up the open air fireside. Meanwhile the men play dominoes or cards and look after the remainder of the rum. In the early

evening the tombstone is placed on the bed and the 'Parent Plate' of food, without salt, is set on a table bedecked with a white cloth, flowers and candles. The drums begin to beat and everyone else is served food with salt picked from the salt pans next to Windward Bay. The celebration resumes with a 'praise' in the night. Family members stay until dawn when they process, singing, to the graveyard to erect the tombstone.

With the growth of tourism in the Caribbean, the Mayreau people set to work to get in on the act. They formed the Mayreau Environmental Development Organisation and, with the able guidance of their turbulent but much loved priest, Fr Mark De Silva,

The Carenage at Salt Whistle Bay is a favourite anchorage for yachts.

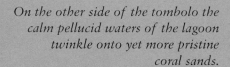

On the other side of the tombolo the calm pellucid waters of the lagoon twinkle onto yet more pristine coral sands.

have developed something that can be held up as a model for sustainable tourism. Each week in the tourist season a windjammer schooner and a yacht or two come into the safe, sandy anchorage of Saline Bay. They enjoy the swimming, snorkel a little perhaps, or go for a stroll ashore. They may visit the Marine Environment Interpretation Centre adjoining the pretty little Roman Catholic Church to find out more about life in the coral gardens and perhaps arrange a half-day tour. There is a super lookout point over the cays from this hilltop site. In the evening, the Mayreau String Band may be invited to play on board. After dinner the holidaymakers are welcomed into the village to join the locals for one drink in each bar as they progress up the hill. At the last bar the whole thing turns into a party and the rhythms of the Caribbean beat out into the wee small hours of the morning. The happy visitors enjoy an unforgettable experience provided by the local people with minimum adverse impact on the environment and a contribution in cash or kind to conservation. This has to be ecotourism at its best!

A watchman looks out for shadows on the surface of the sea which hint at the presence of schools like these. The fishing team is galvanised into action to crew the boats.

Fishing boats are anchored together with the seine in many parts of these islands. This provides a place to preserve the fish live until they are needed.

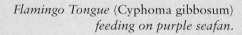

Flamingo Tongue (Cyphoma gibbosum) feeding on purple seafan.

Off limits to the fishermen, the Tobago Cays Marine Park viewed from the church. The dark blues indicate where the Mayreau Garden reefs grow.

7

Aerial close up of Petit Tabac. Not yet in the Marine Park, it is a campsite for Bequia fishermen.

Tobago Cays

A treasure trove of enchanting communities of sea creatures nested amongst a scatter of coral islets.

This school of bluehead wrasse (Thalassoma bifasciatum) *swimming around the barrel sponge are typically the first fish you learn to identify on the reef. The small yellow ones are young and initial phase adults. The 15cm long bluehead is the supermale.*

Tobago Cays

The Tobago Cays include a pattern of four tiny uninhabited islands. They are encircled by the Horseshoe Reef on three sides leaving the western approach open. The islands are arranged around a sandy-bottomed lagoon covered by seagrass beds and mangroves, which act as a nursery for fish and lobsters. Fringing reefs adjoining Jamesby and Petit Bateau are festooned with branching finger corals *(Porites spps)*. Snorkellers and divers could have an impressive encounter with a nurse shark *(Ginglymostoma cirratum)* or a grouper *(Epinephelus spps)* here.

Patch reefs have developed on the underlying platform between these small islands and Mayreau itself to form coral gardens. As divers drift with the current at 12m to 20m depth they may be circled by inquisitive barracuda *(Sphyraena barracuda)* or watch the graceful stingrays *(Urolophus jamaicensis)* go by. Their boat drifts after them obviating the need to anchor in this fragile ecosystem.

The arcuate Horseshoe Reef offers fascinating deeper diving for experts. If they are lucky they may catch a glimpse of the resident 2.4m long jew fish *(Epinephelus itajara)* under an overhang of soft gorgons and coral.

There is a reef a little further east called World's End. Its name intimates the centuries of isolation from human influence, which has produced this superlative marine community. It was in recognition of the special nature of this area that it was designated the Tobago Cays Marine Park. Benchmark studies have begun with the establishment of photoquadrats fixed in the hard coral, the basic building block of the reef. It is important to monitor the amount of coral and the variety of species over time so that we can conserve this pristine environment. The growth of mustard coral *(Porites astreoides)*, a delicate type which suffers when water quality is poor, is a good sign. Soon we hope to have anchor buoys in place where yachts can tie up safely without churning sediment from the seabed. Fortunately most yachting people now have holding tanks for their waste and take their refuse to yacht servicing facilities. The challenge is to keep the reef intact for our children whilst sharing its enchantment with responsible visitors.

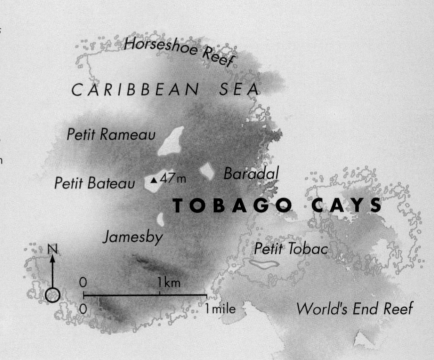

Horseshoe Reef

CARIBBEAN SEA

Petit Rameau

Petit Bateau ▲47m Baradal

TOBAGO CAYS

Jamesby

Petit Tobac

N

0 _____ 1km

0 _____ 1mile

World's End Reef

Beach on Jamesby.

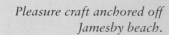

Pleasure craft anchored off Jamesby beach.

Coming in to the beautiful, turquoise lagoon, over Horseshoe Reef, you can see on the right, as though lodged like driftwood on the sand, the isle of Petit Rameau, our 'little branch.' In the centre are the beckoning shores of Baradal with the white beaches of Petit Bateau behind and on the left Little Jamesby. Petit Tabac lies off left. Mayreau can be seen across the coral gardens whilst the misty image of Union Island merges with the horizon.

If you are lucky the shy spotted moray eel (Gymnothorax moringa) *can be seen with its head peeping out from under a coral ledge.*

Brain corals abound.

The Tobago Cays Marine Park is an absolute dream for divers.

Petit Bateau from Jamesby.

The fringing reef of Petit Bateau.

Swimming at Petit Bateau.

Baradal.

If you take a snorkel with you, you could see the peacock flounder (Bothus lunatus) *resting on the sandy bottom. Look carefully; it is a master of camouflage. Can you see the eyes?*

145

The schooner Scaramouche *under sail in the Tobago Cays.*
Drop us off at Union Island please.

Clifton street stalls sell the choicest fruit and vegetables brought down on the Barracuda *mailboat from St Vincent.*

8

Union Island

That most African of islands – practically everyone here is a descendent of people who came from Angola, Cameroon or the Gulf of Guinea.

Whichever way you go it is fish.

Union Island

Union Island, with its distinctive silhouette formed by the Pinnacle, 104m high, is the port of entry in the southern Grenadines. Arriving at the airport you can transfer by boat to Palm Island and Petit St Vincent or take a catamaran tour of the Tobago Cays. It is also the home base for the mailboat, which provides a triweekly service to Kingstown. Links southwards are to Grenada and Trinidad.

There are two towns on this 8.5 square-kilometre island: Ashton and Clifton, both named after suburbs of Bristol. Ashton is the main centre of population for this seafaring people. Those left at home practise subsistence farming in the rainy season based on pigeon peas, corn, peanuts and sweet potatoes. Stock, chiefly goats and sheep, are tethered at this time but when the dry months start in January it is 'let go' season and they forage for what they can get. With rainfall averaging only 1056mm per year, the island is so dry that there are no permanent streams at all. The Amerindians got around this problem by settling at Water Rock on Chatham Bay and Miss Pierre on Richmond Bay, two sites which are swampy and waterlogged all the year round.

Clifton is well known for its sheltered anchorage. It was here that the colonialists arrived, first the French, and in particular a Monsieur Jean Augier and then, in the late eighteenth century, the British, in the person of Samuel Span of Bristol. His family owned a company involved in the triangular trade which linked Union

and the other islands with Britain and probably Cameroon and Angola. He ran Union as a single estate and because of the dry climate he grew cotton. If you climb up to Fort Hill you can still see where cannon once protected Span's settlement near Clifton. Some 10 ponds for water storage and roads for cattle carts date from this time, as does the practice of planting tamarind (*Tamarindus indica*), mango (*Mangifera indica*), sugar apple (*Annona squamosa*) and plum trees (*Spondias monbin*) along the roadsides.

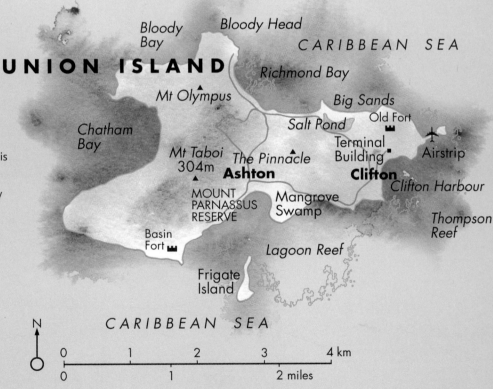

Bloody Bay
Bloody Head
CARIBBEAN SEA
UNION ISLAND
Richmond Bay
Mt Olympus
Big Sands
Salt Pond
Old Fort
Chatham Bay
Mt Taboi 304m
The Pinnacle
Terminal Building
Airstrip
Ashton
Clifton
Clifton Harbour
MOUNT PARNASSUS RESERVE
Mangrove Swamp
Thompson Reef
Basin Fort
Lagoon Reef
Frigate Island

N

CARIBBEAN SEA

0   1   2   3   4 km
0   1   2 miles

We land at Clifton harbour.

The natural vegetation of Union Island has largely been shaved off to accommodate farming. Foraging goats prevent its re-establishment save for the prickliest contenders like the long spined prickly pear (*Opuntia dillenii*) with its pretty lemon flowers and the various species of acacia bush. In the west, however, it is a different story. The slopes of Mount Taboi and Mount Olympus leading down to the Chatham Bay have, in their isolation, regenerated an intriguing secondary dry forest. The Union Island Ecotourism Movement is busy, in collaboration with the Eastern Caribbean Coalition for Environmental Awareness, developing nature trails through the area. Guides will be able to take you past peeling eucalyptus trees (*Busera simaruba*), 15m high, being pollinated by crested hummingbirds. Further along the trail you may come across a manicou apple or a young silkcotton or kapok tree (*Ceiba pentandra*) with its curious bottle shaped trunk encrusted with sharp conical spines. Beware, if you see the 6cm long form of the black pepsis wasp drift across. It will be hunting tarantulas. No need to worry though, these spiders, despite their bad press, are shy and reclusive as far as humankind goes.

Cultural traditions which have their roots in Africa, survived in the small remote islands of the southern Grenadines possibly better than anywhere else in the Caribbean except Haiti. There were very few Whites in Union (under 3 per cent) to feel threatened by what they could have interpreted as witchcraft. As slaves sat deseeding cotton lint they had time to tell stories, reminisce and plan. They developed fishermen's feasts to pray for a good catch and went 'marooning' to invoke the deities to send rain. Perhaps the most colourful festival is the traditional wedding. To the beat of the big drum and calabash shak shak the fathers of the happy couple, each holding a flag, would dance. The bridegroom's father carried a pink flag on a pole. He must outdance the bride's father so that the pink flag always has ascendancy over the white one, which represents the bride. Gradually the dancers meet and the flags unite promoting the couple's union. It is then the women's turn and they perform a similar ritual as they dance the wedding cake, borne in African style on the head. The next 'meeting up' would be at the altar.

'Anyone home?'

Over in Ashton this interesting old creole style house stands side by side with more modern ones. The 'board' upstairs is living accommodation whilst the 'wall' downstairs houses a rum shop and general store. H'mm, I wonder what time they open.

Old Span lands below the Pinnacle are now redistributed.

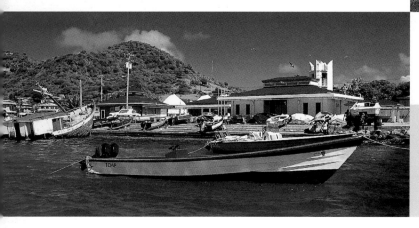

Yesterday, today and tomorrow. Decaying wooden boat grounded as new facilities for fish marketing come on line next to the emerging Marine Park Centre. Both buildings have red 'pagoda' roofs.

Jacks are always popular fried.

Especially with active children.

Looking through the yachts at anchor in Clifton Bay, you can glimpse Palm Island and Petit St Vincent.

And here comes a plane full of holidaymakers heading that way.

Eventually the estate system fell into decline. In 1910 the land was bought out by the Crown and divided up into some 350 parcels of land for sale to Unionites at £4 to £8 per acre. Little was heard again of the planters except for one, Charles Mulzac, a Scot. He remained in Union with his African wife and had a grandson, Captain Hugh Mulzac. He was brought up building boats and whaling. He earned the distinction of being the first 'man of colour' to command a ship of the US Navy in the Second World War.

It was the building of the airstrip in 1974 which opened the way for the export of fish, by air, to Martinique. The reefs and mangrove swamps provide rich feeding grounds for spawning fish as well as offering protection in times of hurricanes. In fact Union Island has the best-developed mangroves in the state. They trap silt and sediment washed down from the hills and the flat coastal land slowly grows. They need protecting.

Today many Vincentians, Caribbean nationals and members of the international yachting community are drawn in to Union for the Easter festivities each year. They enjoy a whole range of sporting and cultural activities culminating in the calypso show.

9

Palm Island

Johnny 'Coconut' Caldwell had a reputation for planting coconut trees wherever he went. Soon Prune Island was nicknamed Palm.

A perfect place for contemplation.

Palm Island

A visit to Prune Island in 1966 would reveal the owners Mary and John Caldwell and their sons newly arrived from Australia. They were still living on board the yacht in which, they had trawled the world's seas looking for the perfect spot to settle. And this coral-fringed island, with the lovely Casuarina Beach, was it. Indeed they never moved again. One might be forgiven, in those days if one had a slightly different perception. As dusk fell a frantic brushing in response to myriads of pin pricks would turn one's arm to carmine, so rampant were the mosquitoes. Even the cows, left to graze there, it was said, would turn tail and swim back to Union Island.

The swamp was drained and palms planted everywhere. A young Swedish construction engineer, struggling for a start in the Caribbean, got the job to design the service complex and villas. He built his own 'eagle's nest' house 60m up on the hilltop. He did such a fine job that his way up the ladder of success was assured. His name was Arne Hasselqvist.

The Palm Island Beach Club opened its doors in December 1967 with 10 rooms, furnished in five duplex bungalows, and a central dining room and lounge. The Caldwells' old yacht charter customers became a loyal clientele in the early days. One or two of them bought house plots and built villas. Over the next 20 years the resort expanded to 24 rooms and 50 building lots were demarcated. The original airstrip with its precarious visual landing was thankfully returned to grass when the Union Island airport opened in 1975. Guests today take the Palm Island ferry across from the airport or arrive by yacht in time for the beach barbecue.

The lovely Casuarina Beach.

Casuarina Beach
Palm Island
Resort

CARIBBEAN SEA

▲17m

PALM ISLAND

N

0   1km

0   1mile

The luck, after all the hard voyaging, was not
to find mosquitoes so bad they drove the cattle
into the sea, nostrils flared and burning;
nor mangrove swamps like quicksand and sandbars like swamp,
the salt pans abandoned and the cotton wild;
but to find the island in the first place
and then, climbing a hill at noon, to see,
surrounded by the ocean and the horseshoe reef,
a small hotel, grasslands and coconut grove.

From *On Palm Island* by Richard Dey.

Native cactus scratch a niche in the cliff overlooking the north coast villas. This is good iguana territory.

The walkway.

And the cool shade under the thatched umbrellas.

A gardener's work is vital in these resort islands.

The restaurant staff are ready
if you have just stopped off
for lunch.

The schooner has come; it is time to go, and there is still more to see.

10

And here we are on the PSV shore. One of those thatched umbrellas looks like it could provide just the sort of cool spot you need for an afternoon snooze.

Petit St Vincent

Ringed by reefs on three sides, PSV, as it is usually called, is approached from the west by boats which ply the waters between Union Island and paradise.

Just outside the cottage door stands the
bamboo flagpole. They say it can bring room
service within seconds so let us try it out.
Take the red flag down, put a little note in the
letterbox, 'I want to be disturbed by a nice cold
beer' and hoist the yellow flag.

Petit St Vincent

PSV was settled by the French who maintained a strong hold on this part of the Grenadines during the colonial period. The island passed to the Church at a point when cash flow was at a low ebb. Subsequently the Roman Catholic Archbishop of Port of Spain returned it to the family. Ms Bethel, a Grenadian who lived in Petit Martinique headed the family at that time. It was Ms Bethel who was to eventually sell the little island to Willis H. Nichols Jr of Cincinnati, Ohio in the 1960s. He formed a company with charter boat owner, Haze Richardson and writer Douglas Terman to develop a resort. Arne Hasselqvist skipped across, flushed with success from Palm Island, and drew up plans. Over the years Haze bought out Douglas Terman's shares and, on the death of Willis, became the sole proprietor.

There is a central service facility and 22 attractive cottages scattered along the shore and up the hillside. The guests are looked after by a staff of 80. The water needs of this upmarket resort are served by solar distillation of sea water. It is hoped that the recent discovery of an aquifer will supplement supplies through a well.

Little more than a kilometre across at most, you can still climb up 40m on Telescope Hill for a panoramic view of what is going on. This is not a bad place to watch the American Thanksgiving weekend yacht races from.

Captain Michael, who hails from Mayreau, sails the Petit St Vincent ferry from Union Island. It is just a breeze away.

But first up to the cottage – the 'picture window' is complimented by the wall of volcanic stone rough hewn from the nearby quarry. Locally made grass mats also feature in the cottages. These can be bought and shipped anywhere in the world, from craft centres in St Vincent.

Meanwhile let us have a look at this cannon. It has no marks but is believed to have come from Petit Martinique so it is probably French.

And through the trees the omnipresent silhouette of Union Island, but what is that in the middle of the sea?

If anything ever goes wrong on Petit St Vincent the mechanic is usually on hand to put it right.

The laughing gulls (Larus atricilla) on the other hand, are not usually around. Their chortling calls can be heard when they come to breed on the remoter rocks from April to September. All the small offshore islands and cays in St Vincent and the Grenadines are protected areas for seabirds.

The unbelievable, archetypal 'desert island' Morpion. They did have a way with words; the French, 'morpion', means crab louse. Morpion has been used as a film set for rum advertisements. However, it currently serves a much more romantic purpose. It is used for weddings and people travel half way across the world to tie the knot in this spot.

And that's how it is with St Vincent and the Grenadines, naval string buried here or not, once it gets in your blood it will draw you back.